Victoria

Wedding Flowers

Victoria

Wedding Flowers

Allison Kyle Leopold
with Gerit Quealy

Hearst Books
A Division of
Sterling Publishing Co., Inc.
New York

Book design by
Alexander Isley Inc.

Copyright © 2003 by Hearst Communications, Inc.

Library of Congress Cataloging-in-Publication Data

Leopold, Allison Kyle.
  Wedding flowers / Allison Kyle Leopold, with Gerit Quealy.
    p. cm.
  ISBN 1-58816-093-9
    1. Wedding decorations. 2. Flower arrangement. 3. Bridal bouquets.
  I. Quealy, Gerit. II. Title.
    SB449.5.W4L46 2003
    745.92'6--dc21   2002155994

10 9 8 7 6 5 4 3 2 1

Published by Hearst Books
A Division of Sterling Publishing Co., Inc.
387 Park Avenue South, New York, NY 10016

🐝 *Hearst Books is proud to continue the superb style, quality, and tradition of* Victoria *magazine with every book we publish. On our beautifully illustrated pages you will always find inspiration and ideas about the subjects you love.*

Victoria is a trademark owned by Hearst Magazines Property, Inc., in USA, and Hearst Communications, Inc., in Canada. Hearst Books is a trademark owned by Hearst Communications, Inc.

Distributed in Canada by Sterling Publishing
c/o Canadian Manda Group, One Atlantic Avenue, Suite 105
Toronto, Ontario, Canada M6K 3E7

Distributed in Australia by Capricorn Link (Australia) Pty. Ltd.
P.O. Box 704, Windsor, NSW 2756 Australia

Manufactured in China.

ISBN 1-58816-093-9

Page 2: *A bouquet of dahlias in brilliant scarlet tones accented with a few pink blooms is a richly romantic and dramatic choice.*

Flowers are Love's truest language.

—Park Benjamin, *Sonnet*

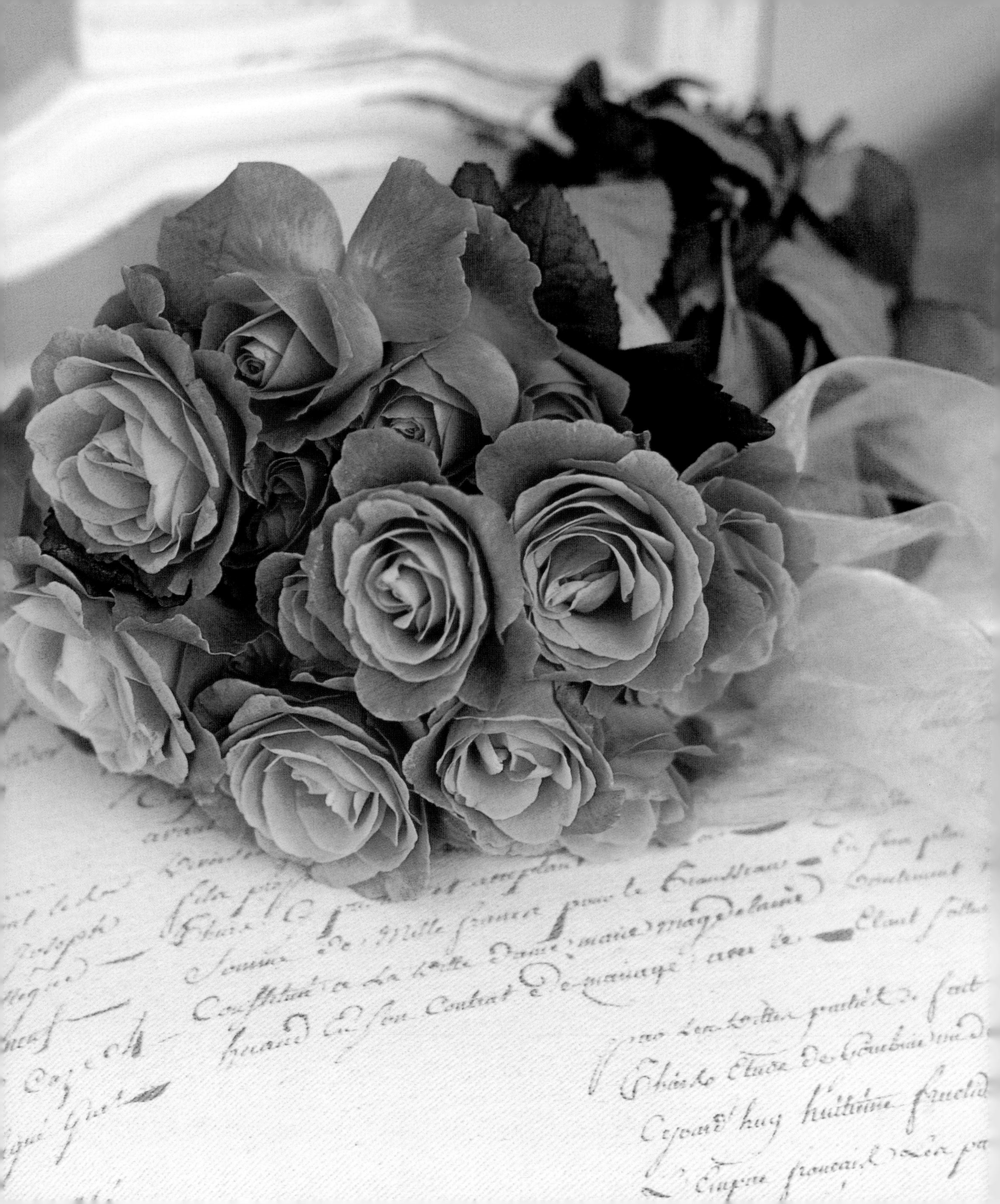

Contents

Introduction

"The wedding day. . . should stand out in the calendar, bright with all the brightness of love and gratitude." Well over one hundred years after these words first appeared in a popular nineteenth-century women's magazine, your wedding day still represents one of the most important milestones of your life, one you'll look back on with fondness for years to come. Even today, it represents the ultimate fantasy—sparkling rings, long white dresses, fresh flowers perfuming the air, your first dance together as husband and wife—all while being surrounded by family and friends, beaming with joy.

The first thing any bride should know about wedding flowers is that they may very well be *the* key consideration in determining the "look" of your wedding.

Like every bride, you naturally want everything about the day to be personal and unforgettable. And whether you're planning an intimate wedding breakfast, a simple buffet, or a formal reception, much of the special charm and romantic atmosphere of your wedding will come from your choice of flowers.

As you go through these pages, you'll find that wedding flowers are much more than mere decorative accessories. Indeed, it's their freshness and vitality that will help you create an event that everyone will remember with pleasure forever. From your own precious bridal bouquet and the flowers for your wedding party to the floral adornments at your ceremony and the centerpieces at your reception, their colors, fragrance and beauty can help transform your wedding day into a magical and momentous occasion.

Opposite: Even if you're planning on wearing a veil, you can still wear flowers on your head. Keep them simple, though, so as not to overwhelm the veil. Here, a single, perfect hydrangea anchors a delicate veil to the bride's hair.

Armfuls of wildflowers and rustic baskets filled with yellow tulips and daisies, for example, immediately call to mind a country wedding. If you've always dreamt of a wedding with a romantic medieval or Victorian theme, you'll likely choose fragrant wreaths of herbs (so suggestive of those days of chivalry) or roses and lacy ferns densely clustered in a nineteenth-century-style bouquet. Specific styles will help give your wedding the period flavor you're looking for. For one celebrity wedding, a renowned floral designer was inspired to re-create the fairy-tale ambience of a glittering turn-of-the-century Russian winter, with a stunning cathedral aisle canopied by twenty-foot snowy white birch trees. Glittering blue lights amidst a "snowfall" of thousands of white flowers pinned to the branches cast an enchanting glow over the ceremony.

In some cases, an affinity for a certain type of flower becomes the theme for the entire wedding. Case in point: the bride-to-be who woke in the middle of the night when a vision of lush, old-fashioned pink roses suddenly appeared in her mind. Absolutely everything, she decided—except for her dress of pure white—would feature those marvelous pink roses, from her bouquet, wedding stationery, and rose-patterned bridesmaids' dresses to minute details like a bit of delicate rose-ribbon trim on her junior bridesmaid's ballet-slipper-style shoes!

On the big day, her dream was realized. Pink roses lavishly embellishing pew ends and doorways greeted guests as they entered the church. At the reception, bowls of pink roses surrounded by twinkling votive candles, long-stemmed roses tucked into folded napkins, and velvety pink petals scattered on tables created an ultraromantic effect. As a crowning touch, even the canapés were flower shaped!

If you're like most brides, though, the prospect of choosing your wedding flowers can be daunting. Unless you routinely order bouquets by the dozen and floral centerpieces for dinners of two hundred, you're soon going to be buying more flowers for one single day than you probably have bought in your entire life! On the other hand, of the myriad decisions you'll face as you progress with your wedding plans, few will be more delightful and fulfilling than deciding on the flowers that best express your love. The very act of planning your wedding flowers tends to give you the opportunity to think about all the tender "little things" that can make a wedding truly unique, from learning what different flowers mean and selecting delicate floral favors for your dearest girlfriends to choosing just the right boutonnieres for the lapels of your husband-to-be and his groomsmen.

So, on the following pages, we're going to demystify the wedding flower process for you. You'll find information on gathering ideas, working with a florist, photographs of traditional (and nontraditional) bouquet styles, a gallery of popular wedding flowers, and much, much more. Plus, we'll take a look at all the many special floral extras that can make your wedding day personal and turn your fantasy into a beautiful reality.

Opposite: *Charmingly old-fashioned, this posy is composed of lilies of the valley and grape hyacinth.*

CHAPTER 1

Flowers, Flowers Everywhere

Flowers are an integral part of your wedding. Chances are you've heard this before, but what does it really mean? To determine that, before you even think about sitting down to talk with a florist, let's consider all the ways, large and small, that flowers enhance—and sometimes actually create—the style and atmosphere of your wedding day.

When people think of wedding flowers, three things generally come to mind: a bridal bouquet, flowers for the wedding party, and the centerpieces. What could be so complex about that? In fact, there are far more opportunities for floral decorations and accessories than you may realize. Most brides today, for example, top their wedding cakes with fresh flowers instead of the conventional plastic bride and groom figures. Cakes themselves are often nestled in a bed of delicate greenery; perhaps a few rosebuds are twisted around the handle of the cake knife that the couple will use to cut the first slice. The bride may want a circlet of traditional orange blossoms to attach to her veil. Or a floral tiara. Or even elegant garland-style headpieces made up of white roses and deep purple anemones for her bridesmaids. Your florist will supply all of these things.

Perhaps you'll need artful greenery and fresh blossoms to transform your reception hall, church, temple, or party tent into a French country garden or Elizabethan fantasy. Or a bower of flowers to decorate a Victorian gazebo. The possibilities are endless. One bride revived a charming old custom she read about in a nineteenth-century etiquette book: A bridesmaid, holding a straw basket filled with long-stemmed flowers, stood at the door of the church handing out flowers to guests as they arrived for the ceremony. Another designed a striking *huppah*—the wedding canopy used in traditional Jewish ceremonies—created entirely from flowers. Perhaps your old college roommate, favorite cousin, or fiancé's parents are coming in from out of town and staying at a local hotel. Many florists will deliver flower baskets coordinated with your wedding theme to their hotel rooms—an especially warm, welcoming touch to greet them when they arrive.

Finally, don't forget about all the surrounding celebrations and events that may call for flowers: bridal showers and engagement parties, wedding breakfasts and rehearsal dinners, your bridesmaid's luncheon, and more.

That's not to say you *must* do all or any of these things. Remember, it's your wedding and your own personal choice. But knowing what the different options are will help you determine how and where you want to feature flowers on your wedding day.

Page 12: *There are more than three thousand varieties of roses. A traditional and romantic choice, roses work well with any style of wedding.*

Wedding Flowers Checklist

Use this checklist as an organizer to help you keep track of the flowers you'll need to order and to help you remain within your budget.

PERSONAL FLOWERS	Quantity	Flower Varieties or Arrangement Style
Bouquets		
Bride	_____	_____
Bride's Tossing Bouquet	_____	_____
Maid/Matron of Honor	_____	_____
Bridesmaid(s)	_____	_____
Junior Bridesmaid(s)	_____	_____
Flower Girl(s)	_____	_____
Boutonnieres		
Groom	_____	_____
Best Man	_____	_____
Groomsmen	_____	_____
Ushers	_____	_____
Father(s)	_____	_____
Ring Bearer(s)	_____	_____
Stepfather(s)	_____	_____
Grandfather(s)	_____	_____
Special Guests	_____	_____

PERSONAL FLOWERS	Quantity	Flower Varieties or Arrangement Style
Corsages		
Mother(s)	_____	_____
Stepmother(s)	_____	_____
Grandmother(s)	_____	_____
Special Guests	_____	_____
Hair Ornaments		
Bride	_____	_____
Maid/Matron of Honor	_____	_____
Bridesmaid(s)	_____	_____
Junior Bridesmaid(s)	_____	_____
Flower Girl(s)	_____	_____
Ceremony		
Entrance	_____	_____
Railing Garlands	_____	_____
Pew/Chair Decorations	_____	_____
Altar Arrangements	_____	_____
Huppah	_____	_____
Petals for Flower Girl	_____	_____
Tossing Petals	_____	_____
(for bride and groom's departure)		

PERSONAL FLOWERS	Quantity	Flower Varieties or Arrangement Style
Reception		
Entryway Arrangements	_____	_____
Place-Card Table Arrangements	_____	_____
Head Table Arrangements	_____	_____
Centerpiece Arrangements	_____	_____
Buffet Table Arrangements	_____	_____
Bar Decorations	_____	_____
Restroom Arrangements	_____	_____
Cake Table Decorations	_____	_____
Wedding Cake Decorations	_____	_____
At-Home Weddings		
Entryway	_____	_____
Mantel Decorations	_____	_____
Window Treatments	_____	_____
Staircase	_____	_____
Home Altar	_____	_____
Chairs	_____	_____

Special Touches

Flowers for Hotel Rooms for Wedding Party and Other Guests

Flowers for the Rehearsal Dinner

Flowers for Decorating the Grill of the Bridal Car

Thank-you Bouquet for the Bride's Parents

Thank-you Bouquet for the Groom's Parents

Getting Started

Traditional or contemporary? White roses or yellow tulips? Gardenias, pansies, freesia, or lilacs? Unless you're a horticultural pro or gardening expert, how do you go about selecting the flowers that best express your personal style?

The first thing to realize is that your choice of flowers *is* personal—there is no right or wrong when it comes to wedding flowers, nor are there any rules you *must* follow. If there is a flower that has a special meaning to you and your groom—perhaps he brought you yellow daisies on your first date—then by all means incorporate it into your wedding theme. Are you worried that using flowers other than traditional pastel-colored blooms will look odd and inappropriate? Perish the thought! Yes, soft yellow, creamy white, and delicate blush-pink blossoms are traditional because they *do* look beautiful at weddings (next to white, even today, pink is still the most popular color for wedding flowers). But so do less conventional, more dramatic shades of scarlet, blazing orange and apricot, cobalt blue, deep wine-red, and other vibrant colors that have become fashionable in recent years. So express yourself. The point is, on this day, your flowers are an expression of who you are and how you see yourselves as a couple. Be as romantic, playful, imaginative, or offbeat as you wish.

Of course, that's not to say there aren't some guidelines to help make your choices easier. While the *style* of your wedding flowers is strictly personal, the month in which you're planning to be married, where you live, your budget, and other factors play a significant part in your final choices.

Arrangements that reflect a contemporary point of view usually use fewer types of flowers and feature a single type in each bouquet.

Expressing Your Personal Style

Think about the weddings you've attended, and chances are your favorites, the ones that stand out in your mind as memorable or moving, are not the biggest, most fashionable, or most extravagant, but rather those that have a certain, elusive "something extra." They don't simply mimic the latest trends or reproduce some designer-of-the-moment's style, but somehow manage to express something personal about the wedding couple's taste and style.

So when it comes to flowers, how do you select those that reflect your personality, your style, and your view of life? That's where your florist comes in. On meeting a new bride-to-be, he or she may make note of certain visual clues to get a sense of your personal style (how you dress, for example, or wear your hair or makeup). He or she may ask you questions about the type of décor you favor, and your reactions to different fragrances (more brides are taking fragrance into account when choosing flowers). But, often, color is the most important element: Your florist will ask you what color flowers you envision (all-white, shades of pink, red, yellow, and orange, etc.) and then tell you what flowers are available in that particular color.

What your wedding gown looks like will also help the floral designer zero in on the

Page 18: *Tulips are available in a wide range of colors, including white, pink, yellow, red, magenta, and purple. They work well for both formal and casual weddings.*

Opposite: *This bride is carrying a whimsical parasol composed of yellow oncidium orchids. Floral touches in imaginative and unusual forms such as this parasol can make your special day even more memorable.*

right flowers for you. If you've always dreamed of floating down the aisle in yards of satin or filmy tulle, with the requisite "something old, something new, something borrowed, and something blue," accordingly, your florist may suggest formal, elegant arrangements of lilies, roses, orange blossoms, and starry bunches of stephanotis. Are you getting married in a slim gown with sleek, modern lines and favor a "less is more" style of décor? So it should be with your flowers—perhaps orchids and arum lilies in cool, spare, Asian-influenced arrangements.

Of course, no one is suggesting you confine yourself to such neat, cookie-cutter categories of "romanticist," "traditionalist," and so on. Most personalities are too complex and eclectic for that. That's why, as you work with your florist, you'll find it is not so much the actual flowers that are important, but how they look together that counts.

The following tips will help you visualize your style in terms of flowers.

The same flowers can express different moods, depending on variety, color, and form. Pink-, peach-, or champagne-colored roses and looser blooms say romantic while Black Magic roses (a velvety, mysterious dark red), vibrant hues, and tighter blooms may feel contemporary or sophisticated, depending on what they are paired with.

Arrangements that reflect a contemporary point of view usually use fewer types of flowers and feature a single type in each bouquet.

Traditional arrangements have a greater variety of different types of flowers per bouquet and often are placed in antique-style or silver containers. A typical combo: all-white or pastel-colored flowers—peonies, calla lilies, sweet peas, and ranunculus.

Loose, unstructured arrangements of flowers with long stems and stalks (such as delphiniums) and old-fashioned, unpretentious flowers like daisies, tulips, cornflowers,

Opposite: Even the family pet can get in on the action. Here, a loyal Labrador stands ready to lead the bridal party to the altar at this home wedding. The color of the dog's collar has been color-coordinated with the hue of the roses.

BIRTH MONTH FLOWERS

January: Carnation
February: Violet
March: Daffodil
April: Sweet Pea
May: Lily of the Valley
June: Rose
July: Larkspur
August: Gladiolus
September: Aster
October: Calendula
November: Chrysanthemum
December: Narcissus

lavender, and Queen Anne's lace suggest a country or garden mood. For bouquets, consider a sheaf style, brimming with berries and herbs. **For an ultraromantic feeling**, go for lush profusions of varied blooms in velvety textures and brilliant colors or monochromatic arrangements. **Choosing flowers by fragrance** can be a lovely idea; that way, whenever you smell lilacs or lavender or gardenias, for example, you'll be reminded of your wedding day. Freesia, roses, gardenias, lilacs, lilies, tuberoses, hyacinths, violets, lavender, and sweet peas are among the most fragrant flowers. If scent is important to you, be aware that while many new hybrid flowers are beautiful, they often have very little or no scent at all.

Practical Considerations

Once you've considered your personal style, you'll have to think about practicalities. Various factors, especially seasonal and budget considerations, may play a role in your choice of flowers, affecting the varieties you choose, the colors, and the quantities.

Seasonal Availability

In the past, brides were restricted to choosing flowers that were in bloom only in their particular area at that particular moment. In fact, many florists still urge you to consider seasonal availability when it comes to wedding flowers. It's not a bad idea, either. There's still something to be said for the freshness and suitability of flowers

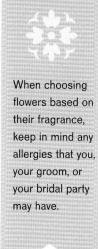

When choosing flowers based on their fragrance, keep in mind any allergies that you, your groom, or your bridal party may have.

that are evocative of the season at hand. Not convinced? Imagine attending a wedding in steamy August where pots of brilliant red poinsettias and boughs of holly line the bridal aisle. Or delicate daffodils and daisies at a wedding on a chilly November eve. Even to a floral novice, these combinations seem unnatural and incongruous, don't they? That's why taking into account some degree of seasonal availability simply makes good sense.

Seasonal availability means more than knowing that tulips bloom in the spring, peonies blossom in May or June, and sunflowers are easier to come by in late July than in deep December. It also depends on local climate. Frosty white roses, mistletoe, and evergreens might sound perfect for a December bride—but only if she lives in New England, not Hawaii. If your wedding is in the summer (or you live in a hot, humid climate all year round), you'll be better off forgoing fragile flowers like gardenias, lilies of the valley, tulips, and wildflowers, for hardier blooms that won't wilt, like sunflowers, zinnias, hydrangeas, and dahlias.

If you have an unlimited budget and can fly in, from anywhere in the world, any out-of-season flower or exotic bloom that strikes your fancy, then by all means,

Left: *In this classic round bouquet, pale pink parrot tulips add a whisper of color to the creamy white French tulips.*

indulge! But if budget is a consideration, you'll quickly realize that locally grown, seasonal flowers will be a lot kinder to your pocketbook. Out-of-season flowers such as imported orchids or white peonies in February will need to be specially ordered and can cost up to three or four times as much as flowers that are locally grown, and some florists insist they find locally grown blossoms fresher than ones that need to be specially ordered. One florist who emphatically prefers local seasonal blooms to forced, hothouse flowers put it this way: Nature produces its best naturally.

But what if there is one exotic or out-of-season flower that you simply have your heart set on for your wedding. If so, go for it—you can cut floral corners elsewhere by going with seasonal greenery and local flowers for everything else. And remember, some flowers—ivy, roses, and evergreens, to name just a few—are year-round favorites and are always stylish, beautiful, and appropriate for weddings.

Although your local florist is your best guide to what flowers are obtainable where you live, this list will give you some general guidelines as to seasonal availability.

Spring: tulips, amaryllis, bluebells, mimosa, lily of the valley, calla lilies, daffodils, forget-me-nots, anemones

Spring to Summer: iris, orchids, clematis, freesia (to late summer), foxglove, gardenias

Spring to Early Fall: stephanotis

Late Spring to Early Summer: peonies, ranunculus, rosemary, lilacs, magnolias (spring to midsummer)

Summer: sunflowers, baby's breath, lavender, larkspur, carnations, Queen Anne's lace

Summer to Fall: hydrangea, snapdragons, heather, dahlias, delphinium

Fall: hydrangea, calla lilies in fall colors, fall roses, pansies

Winter to Spring: camellias, hyacinth, paperwhites, narcissus, daffodils, sweet pea

Opposite: Tulips, pansies, and a large calla lily anchor this loosely arranged sheaf-shaped bouquet of white flowers. While a sheaf shape can be very formal, the mix of flower varieties here gives the bouquet a freshly picked feel.

Calculating Costs

Next to the cost of your reception, your flowers are probably the most expensive item in your wedding budget. As a general rule, whether your wedding costs $5,000 or $50,000, experts advise setting aside about ten to fifteen percent of your overall wedding budget for flowers.

Of course that's just an average, which means that as many people spend more as spend less. If flowers are especially important to you and you've always envisioned yourself surrounded by masses of fresh blooms on your wedding day, you'll want to apportion more money to flowers and less to other areas.

But what do they cost? Before you sit down with your florist, do a little homework on how specific items are priced. Depending on the style, size, and types of flowers you want (and where you live), bridal bouquets can be priced anywhere from $75 to several hundred dollars each. Large or dense arrangements with more flowers or with exotic or out-of-season blooms will obviously cost more.

The list below will help you estimate some typical costs for flowers for your ceremony and reception. Prices will vary from region to region and depend on your choice of flowers, their arrangement, and seasonal availability.

Bridal bouquet: $75 and up

Bridesmaid bouquet: $40 and up

Floral hair wreath: $35 to $100

Corsage: $5 to $25 and up

Boutonniere: $5 to $10

Flowers for your ceremony: $100 to $500 per arrangement

Reception centerpieces: $80 to $250 and up

Floral huppah: $250 to $3,000

Opposite: A single strong color—romantic yellow in this case—makes a lush bouquet and a big impact.

Blooms on a Budget

Following are some strategies to help you keep costs down:

Smart scheduling: When you're choosing a wedding date, remember that flowers (especially roses) are pricier around Valentine's Day, Mother's Day, and other holidays when flowers are more in demand in general. On the other hand, if you are getting married over a holiday, your church already may be decorated with Christmas holly and poinsettias, or Easter lilies, which can cut down or even eliminate the cost of ceremony flowers. You may need only to adorn the pew ends (or the last chair in each row) with ribbon and tulle. The same thing holds true if your ceremony is outdoors, in a park, garden, or on the beach; extra flowers may not be needed at all.

The time/labor factor: Often, it's not the flowers themselves but the florist's labor and time that increase the cost. So think twice about small but potentially expensive details (floral napkin rings that need to be individually wrapped around each napkin, for instance).

Keep it simple: Instead of formally arranged bouquets made with different types of flowers, consider having your bridesmaids carry a simple nosegay or a single flower or two (one perfect calla lily, a sunflower or orchid, a few tulips, or a large-headed rose). At the reception, loose flowers in vases will cost less than elaborately arranged centerpieces.

FLOWERS: WHO PAYS FOR WHAT?

The rule is . . . there are no rules. But if you're following tradition, the bride's family pays for ceremony and reception flowers, and flowers for the bridesmaids and flower girl. The groom pays for the bride's bouquet, although the flowers are chosen by the bride. The groom also pays for boutonnieres for himself, his father, best man, and ushers, and for corsages for his mother and the bride's mother. Corsages and boutonnieres for grandparents on either side are a nice gesture, though not strictly traditional. They, too, are paid for by the groom. The bride's father's boutonniere is traditionally ordered by and paid for by the mother of the bride.

Fool the eye: Use inexpensive flowers and greenery like baby's breath and ivy to add fullness to skimpy bouquets and arrangements. Herbs also will add fullness, texture, and fragrance. A bouquet of fresh mint, rosemary, and marjoram will not only look wonderful, but will also smell wonderful.

Double up: Let bridesmaids' bouquets do double duty. Glass vases placed on the cake table or guest-book table can hold bridesmaids' bouquets at the reception and save you the expense of additional centerpieces.

Far left and near left: Some brides opt to include beaded flowers in their bouquets. This exuberant bouquet includes roses in the palest shade of pink, white peonies, and a few delicate beaded flowers.

Recycle: After the ceremony, have the altar flowers and decorations moved to your reception (pew decorations can be draped on doors or buffet tables; altar arrangements on the dais or cake table). Similarly, if you're having a wedding brunch the next morning, consider reusing the reception centerpieces. Otherwise, have them delivered to the hotel rooms of out-of-town guests so they can continue to be enjoyed, or donate them to a hospital, community shelter, retirement home, or charity event.

Use interesting containers: Choose containers and vases that look pretty with just a few select flowers, rather than elaborate, costly arrangements. Consider rustic wooden boxes or terra-cotta pots instead of cut-glass vases, or scour flea markets, thrift stores, and tag sales for interesting unmatched vintage vases at minimal cost. Be creative: For a country wedding, for example, try a cluster of glass tumblers, old-time preserving jars, or glass milk bottles filled with flowers on your tables. Discount shops can also offer up attractive surprises—and bargains—such as milk glass vases, small pitchers, and the like.

Add accessories: Let accessories add ambience to your reception tables without upping costs. Supplement small or simple flower arrangements with votive candles, candlesticks in varying heights, baskets of moss, and bowls of fruit and nuts.

Break 'em away: Arrange small pots of flowering plants together to form what are known as "breakaway" centerpieces. Afterward, guests take them home as wedding favors.

Watch the whites: White flowers may be traditional, but they cost more than colored flowers. Because white flowers bruise easily, your florist will need to buy more than are called for to replace any that may be damaged from handling.

Your Ceremony and Reception Sites

Spend some time at the sites you've chosen for the ceremony and the reception. Do you want to highlight their special features (especially if the architecture of the

Opposite: Utilitarian objects can be used in witty new ways. Simple or quirky containers, for example, from nurseries, tag sales, or even hardware stores make attractive, original, and affordable centerpieces for the bride on a budget. This small galvanized-steel tub brimming with flowers makes an ideal centerpiece for a casual summer wedding.

venue is designed in a particular architectural style, such as Arts and Crafts or English Tudor), or transform them completely? A reception at your local country club may require a lot of flowers to enliven a humdrum room, whereas a grand hotel ballroom may call for just a few elegant arrangements. If your wedding will be held outdoors, the beauty of the site may be enough to set a romantic mood; in that case, you might just need a few floral decorations at the outdoor "altar."

Gathering Ideas

After you've locked in your wedding date, it's a good idea to start a wedding notebook. Most brides choose a scrapbook-style journal in which to paste or tape pictures or an oversized loose-leaf binder set up with dividers and zippered inserts to hold fabric swatches and sundries. Unless you're highly knowledgeable about flowers, you may not be able to describe the type of arrangements you envision, or even identify the specific flowers in a bouquet you've fallen in love with. But having photographs of flowers or arrangements you like is a great way to help your wedding planner or florist effectively hone in on the mood and look you want.

In your notebook, then, set aside a section designated "Flowers" and start collecting ideas. Tear out pictures that appeal to you from magazines; include photographs of place settings, centerpieces, and bouquets that you like (or ones you don't). Collect suggestions for floral favors that seem unique, ideas from other weddings you've attended, and more. Talk to your friends (especially those who are recent brides) about weddings they've attended where the flowers were especially notable.

Over the next few weeks, assembling these examples will give you some familiarity with the subject. At some point, you may notice a common thread in the type of flowers you're drawn to, be it color, texture, or overall style. Perhaps your pages are filled with simple, loosely arranged flowers with a "just-picked-from-the-garden" look, as opposed to formal, elaborately wired arrangements. Try to keep a small camera in your purse when you're going out shopping or attending another event (it doesn't have to be a wedding); you never know when you'll pass a store window or attend a party that has a centerpiece or flower arrangement you want to remember.

ANEMONE

Season: November–May

Colors: white, pink, purple, magenta, burgundy

Cost: moderate to expensive

Scent: none

ASTER

Season: November–May

Colors: white, yellow, pink, purple

Cost: moderate

Scent: none

AMARYILLIS

Season: November–April

Colors: white, green, yellow, pink, red, burgundy

Cost: moderate to expensive

Scent: none
(the belladonna variety, shown here, has a mild fragrance)

Popular Wedding Flowers

To help you familiarize yourself with the countless varieties flowers come in, following is a visual guide organized in alphabetical order. This is not a complete list; rather, it highlights flowers that are popular for weddings. Each flower has its own special qualities, whether it's color, shape, or fragrance. As you browse through these pages, you'll see old favorites and discover new ones, and you'll gain a better sense of which blooms appeal to you.

CALLA LILY

Season: year-round; peak is winter to late spring

Colors: ivory, yellow, orange, pale pink, dark pink, red, burgundy

Cost: expensive

Scent: none

CANTERBURY BELLS

Season: June–October

Colors: white, blue, purple, pink

Cost: expensive

Scent: none

CHRYSANTHEMUM

Season: year-round; peak in late summer and fall

Colors: white, yellow, green, orange, russet, red, burgundy

Cost: inexpensive

Scent: musky

CAMELLIA

Season: late winter to early spring; fall

Colors: white, cream, pink, red

Cost: inexpensive to moderate

Scent: sweet

CORNFLOWER

Season: summer to early fall

Colors: white, pink, blue

Cost: inexpensive to moderate

Scent: none

COSMOS

Season: midsummer to fall

Colors: white, pale pink, dark pink

Cost: inexpensive to moderate

Scent: none

DAFFODIL

Season: spring or fall

Colors: yellow, white, apricot, orange

Cost: inexpensive to moderate

Scent: sweet or none

DAHLIA

Season: summer to early fall

Colors: white, yellow, orange, pink, red, purple

Cost: inexpensive

Scent: strong and spicy

DAISY

Season: summer to early fall

Colors: white

Cost: inexpensive

Scent: none to faint

DELPHINIUM

Season: year-round; peak is June–October

Colors: white, lavender, pink, blue, purple

Cost: moderate to expensive

Scent: none

DUTCH TULIP

Season: November–May

Colors: white, yellow, orange, pink, red, purple

Cost: inexpensive to moderate

Scent: none

FORGET-ME-NOT

Season: May–September

Colors: white, blue, pink

Cost: moderate to expensive

Scent: none

FREESIA

Season: year-round

Colors: all colors except blue

Cost: moderate

Scent: sweet

FRENCH TULIP

Season: November–May

Colors: ivory, pale yellow, pink

Cost: expensive

Scent: none

GARDENIA

Season: year-round

Color: ivory

Cost: expensive

Scent: fragrant

GERBERA DAISY

Season: year-round

Colors: white, pink, yellow, orange, red

Cost: moderate

Scent: none

GLADIOLUS

Season: year-round; peaks during the summer

Colors: white, yellow, green, apricot, orange, pink, red, lavender, purple

Cost: inexpensive

Scent: none

GRAPE HYACINTH

Season: November–May

Colors: white-green, blue-purple

Cost: moderate to expensive

Scent: sweet

HYACINTH

Season: November–May

Colors: white, yellow, pale pink, peach, fuchsia, lavender, purple, blue

Cost: moderate

Scent: very sweet

HYDRANGEA

Season: July–November

Colors: white, green, pink, burgundy, purple, blue

Cost: moderate to expensive

Scent: none

IRIS

Season: year-round; peaks in spring to early summer

Colors: white, yellow, purple

Cost: inexpensive to moderate

Scent: none to sweet

LILAC

Season: spring

Colors: white, pale pink, dark pink, lavender, purple

Cost: moderate to expensive

Scent: strong and sweet

LILY

Season: year-round; peaks in spring and summer

Colors: white, yellow, apricot, orange, dark pink, red, purple

Cost: moderate to expensive

Scent: none to strong; depends on variety

LILY OF THE VALLEY

Season: year-round; peaks in spring

Colors: white

Cost: expensive

Scent: fragrant

PEONY

Season: spring

Colors: white, cream, peach, pink, burgundy

Cost: moderate to expensive

Scent: sweet to aromatic

PHLOX

Season: June–November

Colors: white, pink, red, purple, orange

Cost: moderate

Scent: sweet and mild

ORCHID

Season: year-round

Colors: white, yellow, apricot, orange, green, pale pink, dark pink, red, burgundy

Cost: moderate to expensive

Scent: none to fragrant; depends on variety

RANUNCULUS

Season: November–April

Colors: white, yellow, apricot, orange, pink

Cost: moderate to expensive

Scent: mild

ROSE

Season: year-round

Colors: white, cream, yellow, apricot, orange, pale pink, dark pink, red, russet, burgundy, lavender

Cost: moderate to expensive

Scent: none to very fragrant

STEPHANOTIS

Season: year-round

Colors: white

Cost: expensive

Scent: slight

SUNFLOWER

Season: May–November

Colors: deep gold, orange, rus-set, brown, pale lemon

Cost: moderate

Scent: none

SWEET PEA

Season: November–June

Colors: pink, lavender, white, cream, apricot, red, purple

Cost: moderate to expensive

Scent: very sweet

VERONICA

Season: year-round

Colors: white, pink, purple

Cost: inexpensive to moderate

Scent: none

ZINNIA

Season: June–September

Colors: yellow, green, orange, pink, red

Cost: inexpensive

Scent: none

CHAPTER 3

Finding a Florist

When you've reached the point where you have some ideas about the types of flowers you want, the next step is to find a floral designer who can help you achieve your vision. This is the person who will provide all the personal flowers for your wedding as well as create the floral decorations for your ceremony, reception, and any other parties too. Top floral designers and wedding planners are often booked months in advance—sometimes more than a year. (Remember: There are only fifty-two weekends a year and even the most accomplished can only handle so many parties on each weekend.) Be sure to give yourself plenty of time—at least six months to a year before your wedding date—to find a person with whom you're comfortable, who is both creative and able to work within your budget.

If you're not working with a wedding coordinator, the best way to find a talented floral designer is by word-of-mouth. Talk to recently married friends and ask relatives or coworkers for their recommendations as well. If you're at a wedding or other

Page 44: *A bouquet of roses is a classic choice for a bride. This loosely composed arrangement has a fresh, "just picked" look.*

event and think the flowers are fabulous, don't be shy: get the florist's name from your host. Your caterer or reception site manager will have worked with many different florists and often can provide recommendations (anyone they know is likely to be familiar with the wedding site too).

Once you have a few names, ask for Web sites where you can view samples of their work. Many florists will post photographs of different bouquets, centerpieces, and other treatments they have done, so you can immediately get a sense of their style and learn something about their business too. One thing you'll want to learn is how much of their business involves weddings; that way, you know they'll be familiar with any situations that may occur and be able to handle the unexpected. But don't just rely on pictures. Be sure to get references from the florists' previous clients too.

By the time you are ready to interview florists, you should have decided on the date and location of your wedding and, ideally, have chosen your wedding gown. You should have an idea of your budget and have in hand pictures of bouquets and arrangements that illustrate

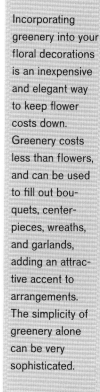

Incorporating greenery into your floral decorations is an inexpensive and elegant way to keep flower costs down. Greenery costs less than flowers, and can be used to fill out bouquets, centerpieces, wreaths, and garlands, adding an attractive accent to arrangements. The simplicity of greenery alone can be very sophisticated.

what you like and what you don't as well as fabric swatches and Polaroids of your wedding gown and attendants' gowns, and sketches, photographs, or floor plans of where your ceremony and reception will take place.

Before setting up consultations, it's helpful to narrow down your list of prospective florists by conducting a brief interview with each over the telephone. A "get acquainted" call will allow you to determine whether or not they're available on your wedding date, whether you have a rapport and will feel comfortable working with them, and what their individual style and experience are. Stay organized by keeping a record of their responses.

Opposite: Many brides opt to use color in their floral decorations, either as an accent to white flowers or as the predominant hue.

Above: If you're having an outdoor wedding, be sure to look around the site for places to use greenery or flowers. Here's a good use of greenery—this heart is composed solely of lemon leaves.

Above: *White flowers may be traditional, but they're more expensive than colored flowers. Because white flowers bruise easily, your florist will need to buy more than are called for to replace any that may be damaged from handling.*

Opposite: *Transform a generic rented chair into something special by trimming it with a garland that matches the bridal party bouquets and centerpieces. Decorating all of the reception chairs with flowers can be quite expensive, so consider reserving this special treatment for the chairs at the wedding party table only.*

Questions to Ask While Interviewing Florists over the Telephone

1. Is my wedding date available?
2. Do you charge a consultation fee?
3. What is your design style? Romantic, modern, minimal?
4. How many weddings have you produced flowers for?

Once you've determined which florists you'd like to meet with, schedule consultations with them. The consultations will allow you to get to know the florists and their work, and to discuss your ideas for your wedding. As you interview different florists, remember that you're there not only to look at the florist's portfolio of wedding arrangements but also to determine if he or she is someone you can communicate with and with whom you feel a rapport. Try to meet two or three florists, even if you feel sure you've found the right one. Prepare for the meetings by gathering magazine photos of flowers and arrangements that you like, a list of your favorite flowers, a checklist of arrangements that you think you'll need (see pages 15–17). If you have them, bring fabric swatches of your and your bridesmaids' gowns so that the florist can suggest complementary colors. Be prepared to discuss the budget as well. (Tip: Don't be shy about discussing the budget. If cost is a concern, ask about less expensive alternatives to flowers that are out of your price range. A professional florist will be able to work with any budget.) The better prepared you are, the better the meeting will go. Your ability to communicate your vision of the wedding will be a key component in work-

FLORAL GLOSSARY

You know what you want, but you don't know what it's called. That's the situation many brides find themselves in when it comes to flowers. Or, you don't know what you want and you need help wading through the field of floral terms to be able to explain with confidence what it is you imagine. Here's a glossary of terms to help your vocabulary blossom.

Boutonniere: A single bloom or bud (or several small buds) attached to the left lapel of the jacket. The men in your wedding party—the groom, best man, ushers, and the fathers of the bride and groom—wear these.

Buttonhole: Another name for boutonniere.

Candelabrum: A floral centerpiece created at the base, neck, or top of a multiarmed candelabrum. Such a centerpiece is usually accented with flowing greens or silk ribbons, depending on the style of the wedding.

Circlet: A floral wreath used as a headdress for the bride, bridesmaids, or flower girls that nestles at the top of the head or is placed mid-forehead.

Corsage: A single bloom or small cluster of blooms sometimes arranged against a lace or tulle doily and/or accented with ribbon. Corsages come in pin-on, wrist, and handheld styles and are typically worn by mothers and grandmothers and other special people not in the wedding party. Orchids and gardenias are popular choices.

Dais: The centerpiece at the head table where the bride and groom are seated. (The table itself also is called the dais.) This floral arrangement usually drapes over the front of the table for visual effect.

Fish Bowl: A low centerpiece style that consists of flowers clustered in a glass bowl.

Floral Foam: Special foam used in flower arrangements. The foam fits in a bouquet holder and retains water like a sponge, hydrating flowers for extended time periods.

Garden: A centerpiece featuring abstract wildflowers. The composition is generally airy and less full than other designs. Lisianthus, hollyhock, rambling roses, digitalis, herbs, and smilax are well suited to this style.

Garland: An elaborately woven rope or strand arrangement typically used to adorn pews and doorways. Garlands also can be held by two or three children and paraded down the aisle.

Hoop: Similar to a wreath and carried by bridesmaids and flower girls.

Ikebana: Japanese-style flower arrangements that are aesthetically in harmony with their surroundings.

Pomander: A bloom-covered ball suspended from a ribbon handle that is carried by brides-maids instead of a bouquet, hoop, or basket. These fragrant and unusual adornments, popular in Victorian England, are ideal for child attendants and make especially pretty keep-sakes after the wedding.

Sprig: A small cluster of blooms or a small stem of leaves or flowers taken from a larger stem or branch.

Taped and wired: A technique for arranging bouquets, boutonnieres, headpieces, and wreaths. The head of a flower is cut from the stem and attached to a wire, which is then wrapped with floral tape. Taping and/or wiring flowers makes it easier to maneuver flowers into the shapes and styles you want.

Topiary: Flowers or foliage trimmed into geometric shapes often resembling miniature trees, spheres, animals, or other forms.

Trellis: A woven wooden frame used as a screen or support for climbing plants and flowers.

Wreath: A ring of flowers or other decorative materials that can function as a centerpiece, headpiece, or door hanger.

FINDING A FLORIST

ing with your florist. Working successfully with a florist usually involves some give and take (especially if, like many brides, you aren't sure exactly what you want). That's where the florist's artistry, creativity, and expertise come in. The right floral designer will not only answer your questions but listen to your concerns, come up with different options, and be sensitive to your likes and dislikes. After all, it's only by talking with you that he or she will be able to make your flowers truly personal.

If the florist has done weddings at your site before, he or she should be able to show you pictures of how they looked and tell you why certain colors, shapes, or styles work (or don't) in that space. Especially if you're a floral novice, he or she should be willing to explain what flowers go together. For example, delicate, ruffled flowers such as sweet peas don't blend well with bold sunflowers or with dramatic, angular tropical flowers such as birds of paradise. Just remember that the florist has to take in the whole picture: the month your wedding will take place, the time of day, the expected weather, the room size, lighting, your dress, market availability of different flowers, *and* your taste and budget.

Questions to Ask During the Consultation with Your Florist

1. Can you show me photographs of your work?
2. What flowers will be in season?
3. How can I make the most of my budget?
4. Have you done weddings at my ceremony and/or reception site before?
5. Will you work on my wedding flowers personally or will your staff do the work?
6. Will you be at the site on my wedding day making sure everything is in order?
7. How many weddings will you be doing on the same day as mine?
8. Do you require a deposit? Is it refundable?

Opposite: *The bride's vibrantly colored bouquet contrasts beautifully with her simple white dress, while her attendants' dresses and bouquets turn the color scheme around: bright red dresses with small bouquets where white flowers are the star.*

THE LANGUAGE OF FLOWERS

The Victorians popularized the language of flowers, whereby different meanings were attributed to different flowers and used as secret messengers of affection. The language of flowers was used by courting couples during the nineteenth century, a time when expressing certain thoughts outright would have been considered forward and improper. Thus, bouquets became imbued with secret sentiments determined by the choice and arrangement of flowers so lovers could impart messages to their dear ones through floral arrangements alone. One arrangement of flowers could propose marriage; another could accept or decline that proposal. Suitors could be encouraged or discouraged and even assignations arranged, all with the sending of the proper posy.

Although many of these floral meanings have long been forgotten, using the language of flowers can be a charming way for you to add a personal meaning to your ceremony.

Below is a sampling of flowers and their traditional meanings.

Amaryllis—Beautiful but timid; pride

Ambrosia—Love returned

Apple Blossom—Preference

Aster—Variety

Azalea—Romance

Bachelor's Button—Hope; single blessedness

Bluebell—Constancy

Buttercup—Riches

Calla Lily—Feminine beauty; modesty

Camellia—Gratitude

Camellia, Red—Loveliness

Camellia, White—Unpretending excellence

Chrysanthemum, Red—I love you

Chrysanthemum, White—Truth

Clover, White—I promise

Cowslip—Pensiveness; winning grace

Dahlia—Dignity and elegance

Daffodil—Unequaled love

Daisy, White—Innocence

Forget-Me-Not—Do not forget; true love

Four-Leaf Clover—Be mine

Fuchsia—Taste or frugality

Geranium—I prefer you; bridal favor

Geranium, Scarlet—Comfort

Heliotrope—Devotion

Hibiscus—Delicate beauty

Honeysuckle—The bond of love

Hyacinth—Constancy

Iris—A message for thee

Ivy—Friendship; fidelity

Lilac—First emotions of love

Lily of the Valley—Return of happiness

Marigold—Sacred affection

Morning Glory—Affection

Orange Blossom—Chastity; purity

Pansy—The thoughts of lovers

Peony—Bashfulness

Periwinkle, White—Pleasures of memory

Primrose—Early youth

Ranunculus—You are radiant with charms

Rose, Red—Love

Strawberry Blossom—Foresight

Sweet Basil—Good wishes

Sweet Pea—A meeting; delicate pleasures

Sweet William—Gallantry

Tulip, Red—Declaration of love

Verbena, Pink—Family union

Violet—Faithfulness, modesty

Water Lily—Purity of heart

Wisteria—I cling to thee

Zinnia—Thoughts of absent friends

The right florist will not only answer your questions but listen to your concerns, come up with different options and be sensitive to your likes and dislikes.

When you've narrowed your choices down to two or three florists, ask for a written estimate of what you've discussed. If you're having trouble making up your mind, it's acceptable to ask the florist to create a sample centerpiece or bouquet. Generally, there will be no extra charge for this service, although it's best to ask about your florist's policy first.

Once you've decided to work together, your florist will set aside your wedding date and draw up a contract. Over the next few months, you will probably meet again several times (more if the florist is providing flowers for your cake, headpieces for your bridesmaids, and other extras). At these meetings, he or she will show you centerpiece containers, finalize the placement of the ceremony flowers, and discuss other details.

Florist Contracts: What You Need to Know

Your contract or letter of agreement should nail down all the specifics you've talked about: every item, fee, date, and delivery. Getting everything spelled out ahead of time will help avoid confusion on the day of your wedding. If you've lined up your florist far in advance of your wedding, it's a good idea to call occasionally in the months before the actual event to make sure that everything is proceeding on schedule.

HERE'S WHAT YOUR CONTRACT SHOULD INCLUDE

Your name, address, and phone number and the florist's name, address, and phone number.

The name of the person with whom you've made the arrangements and the date of your appointment.

A detailed description of each service to be provided. This means the colors, types, and number of flowers in all your arrangements; the number of arrangements; and any items, such as trellises or accessories. Be sure to include an itemized list of prices.

A substitution clause in case your flowers aren't available on your wedding day. This is a list of substitute flowers in your price range that you find acceptable, so there are no unhappy surprises.

Delivery fees for all the flowers, where they should be delivered, as well as the time and date. For example, bouquets and boutonnieres may go to your home; other flowers to the ceremony and reception sites.

The total amount due, the amount of your deposit, and a payment schedule. You may be asked to put down as much as half the total. (Be sure to get a receipt.) The balance may be due anywhere from a few days to a few weeks before the wedding.

Any setup, breakdown, or overtime charges; insurance provided; rental charges (for special vases and other containers); breakage or damage policies and costs; taxes, gratuities, or other additional fees.

The last date that changes are possible as well as the florist's cancellation or refund policy if you have to cancel or if for any reason the florist is unable to provide you with what the contract calls for.

Finally, make sure you retain a copy of the original agreement, with any changes or additions signed or initialed by both you and the vendor, and put it in your wedding notebook or other safe place.

CHAPTER 4

Bouquets

Your bridal bouquet is one of the most important floral elements of your wedding. Year after year, women all over the world walk down the aisle carrying their own choice of carefully selected, artfully assembled flowers. So strongly ingrained is the tradition of the bridal bouquet that even the woman who marries in jeans and T-shirt will still be carrying some kind of flowers. More so than a wedding gown, it's the bouquet that makes her a bride.

Throughout history, brides have carried bouquets to the altar, one of the many wedding rituals that have been associated with flowers. In some early cultures, it was the custom for brides to carry flowers mixed with strong herbs (such as garlic or chives) to ward off evil spirits and prevent bad luck. Sprinkling flower petals in the bride's path as she walks down the aisle originated from the idea of protecting her from evil spirits who dwell below ground.

It was the Victorians, in particular, who gave us many of the wedding traditions still practiced today, especially those that involve flowers. Victorian brides were the

first to marry in white and as noted earlier, it was Victorian lovers who, during courtship, popularized the romantic language of flowers. A bridal bouquet made only from pure white flowers was yet another Victorian custom, one that flourished throughout the twentieth century and is still popular today. So, too, was the creation of a good luck bell (or horseshoe or other lucky symbol) also made entirely of white flowers. These were traditionally suspended over the spot where the bride and groom would stand together at the altar.

Wedding bouquets range from the sublimely simple to the lushly elegant. The most traditional are composed of all white or near-white flowers. This incredibly beautiful and popular look suits any kind of wedding, formal or informal alike. White roses, stephanotis, or all-white lilies of the valley for example, combined with some green foliage, have a timeless elegance. Even common white baby's breath can look starry and spectacular when carried on its own, worn with a simple gown and headpiece. (Tip: It's

Page 58: Red, purple, yellow, and orange come together to create this sumptuous bouquet. The vivid palette was inspired by the bride's embroidered wedding shoes.

Opposite: Sprays of buds and berries in rich red and cranberry tones combined with roses add opulence to a winter wedding.

Left, above: This elegant presentation, or pageant, bouquet consists of white roses with a lovely mix of greenery to round out the arrangement.

Left, below: By including sprigs of herbs, ivy, and ferns, this bouquet is filled with botanical symbols of marital health and happiness. Herbs have played a role in weddings throughout history, representing a variety of good wishes for the bride and groom.

Opposite: This formal bouquet is composed of roses, calla lilies, and gardenias surrounded by dark green leaves. Gardenias have an exquisite fragrance, but are delicate and bruise easily.

Right: The tissue-pink Oceana roses in this bride's nosegay perfectly complement the pale pink silk rosettes on her gown. The sheer pink ribbon adds a flourish of color.

Below: A sumptuous bouquet of lavender roses. In the Victorian language of flowers, lavender roses symbolize enchantment.

also inexpensive, long-lasting, and dries beautifully.) Other popular white bridal flowers are ranunculus, gardenias, calla lilies, orchids, hydrangeas, freesia, and Madonna lilies.

Bouquets that contrast different floral shapes, colors, and textures also are popular, such as traditional roses with peonies, hydrangea, and sweet peas. Flowers in offbeat or unusual colors such as mango, fuchsia, and purple can be especially appealing at casual weddings, while a bride who marries in a beachside ceremony might carry a bouquet adorned with tiny starfish or sea shells. Are you intrigued by the idea of adding herbs to your bouquet? Try a combination of geranium leaves, lemon thyme, basil, lavender, and mint.

The style and flowers chosen for the bride's bouquet set the theme for all the personal flowers for your wedding. Usually it's only after the bridal bouquet has been chosen that flowers are selected for the rest of the wedding party, so that they complement but don't overshadow the bridal bouquet in style, flower selection, and color.

Bouquet Shapes

Bouquets come in many different shapes. Here's a list of classic bouquet shapes for the bride and other members of the bridal party.

POSY

Smaller than nosegays but similar in design, posies have an old-fashioned feel. They work best with smaller blooms, although a few large flowers, such as peonies, can make a statement. Posies are often chosen for bridesmaids or flowers girls. Here, yellow roses and anemones make up this bride's charming posy.

BIEDERMEIER

Also called a ring bouquet, Biedermeier bouquets are a more formal variation of the round bouquet. They are composed of tightly arranged concentric circles of various multicolored flowers. The blooms are wired into a holder, with one flower variety per ring. This Biedermeier is designed with creamy tulips in the center, surrounded by muscari, with ivory roses forming the outside ring.

POMANDER

A ball of flowers suspended from the wrist by a decorative ribbon handle. A sweet alternative for junior bridesmaids and flower girls.

HAND-TIED

Bouquets arranged and held in the hand with the body of the flowers facing upward as if they had been picked fresh from the garden. The stems are wrapped with ribbon and may include a bow accent. This one features roses, hyacinths, lilies of the valley, and other small white blooms.

PRESENTATION (OR SHEAF)

A collection of long-stemmed flowers held in the crook of the arm, typically tied together with ribbons. This presentation bouquet composed of long-stemmed roses tied with a lavender ribbon makes a simple yet elegant bridal bouquet.

ROUND

Similar in style to a nosegay but larger, the round bouquet is ideal for any style of wedding. Here, an abundance of white roses punctuated with a few green leaves make up a classic round bouquet.

CASCADE (OR SHOWER)

A luxurious and formal style, cascades have a waterfall-like spill of blooms, often composed of ivy and long-stemmed flowers, wired to flow (or cascade) over the bride's hands. Light, graceful flowers work best in cascades. This cascade bouquet is designed with white roses and stephanotis.

NOSEGAY

Small, simple, circular bouquets composed of densely packed round flowers, greenery, and occasionally herbs. A versatile shape, nosegays are wired together and anchored in bouquet holders, or tied together. A typical small nosegay might include baby rosebuds, violets, and bachelor's buttons; a larger, looser one might be composed of narcissus and orchids, or old-fashioned roses, such as the nosegay shown here.

HOW TO HOLD YOUR BOUQUET

Before the big day, take time to practice walking while holding your bouquet properly (use a stand-in, such as a book, or buy some flowers to practice with) so that you best feature both the bouquet and your dress as you walk down the aisle. Stand in front of a mirror to check your form; be sure that you're not obscuring your dress or holding the bouquet too low (in which case no one will see your beautiful flowers). If you'll be escorted down the aisle by another person (or two people), practice linking arms with them while holding your bouquet.

Handheld Bouquet: Hold your wrists just above your hipbones and use both hands to hold the stems of the bouquet in front of your belly button. Point your elbows out a little bit, to reveal the curve of your waist and show off your dress.

Presentation Bouquet: Rest the bouquet on the lower part of your arm; don't hold it too closely or you'll risk crushing it.

Other Bouquet Shapes

Composite: A bouquet that uses petals from one or several flowers creating the illusion of a single, oversized bloom.

Spray Bouquet: A triangular-shaped cluster of flowers.

Tussy Mussy: From the Victorian era, a tussy mussy is a posy carried in a small, metallic (often silver or silver-plated) ornamental holder.

Bouquet Tips

Here are a few tips to keep in mind when considering bouquet shapes and styles.

Your bridal bouquet is an accessory that should enhance but not overshadow your gown. Remember to bring a swatch of your wedding gown fabric with you when you choose your bouquet, along with a sketch or photograph of the gown itself.

Add sentimental meaning to your wedding and honor your mother by carrying a bouquet made up of the same flowers she carried (or your grandmother carried). And remember to write down what they are so your own daughter can continue the tradition. (By the way, make a copy of that list for your husband. That way, he can send you the same bouquet on your first anniversary, and every year thereafter!)

Keep proportion—yours and your gown's—in mind when choosing the bouquet style you want. Taller brides can carry larger, cascading bouquets; if you're small, you'll look more natural with a smaller bouquet.

If there's an embellishment on your gown that you want to be seen, discuss it with your florist and ask him or her to recommend a suitable bouquet style.

The bigger, fuller, and more formal your dress, the bigger, fuller and more formal your bouquet should be.

Be sure that your bouquet is easy to carry—neither too heavy nor too cumbersome. You want to walk down the aisle with grace and ease, and not worry about fussing with or handling your flowers.

Don't overlook the importance of greenery and foliage in your bouquet. Lacy ferns, ivy, and other greens can provide a wealth of textures and even different colors (like soft brown-greens, deep green, and rich bronze shades, or the silvery tones of Dusty Miller).

Keep the mood of your bouquet in harmony with the formality of the affair. A bouquet of fresh green wheat and wildflowers suits a country wedding, not a white-tie reception.

If you're carrying lilies, be sure your florist removes the stamens to prevent pollen from staining your dress.

Opposite: To complement the bride's wedding gown, the floral designer created a nosegay of soft, fully open pink and lavender roses spiked with maroon buds.

Left: Creamy white roses mixed with white and lavender hydrangeas comprise this traditional round bouquet.

CHAPTER 5

Flowers for the
Wedding Party

Traditionally, flowers for the wedding party include bouquets
for the bridesmaids and maid and matron of honor, a basket
of flowers for the flower girl, corsages for the mothers of the
bride and groom, and boutonnieres for all the men—the groom,

the fathers, the best man, the ushers, and even the ring bearer. Flowers can be ordered
for other specials guests as well, such as stepparents, grandparents, and godparents.

Bridesmaids, Mothers, and Flower Girls

Bouquets for the women in the bridal party take their cue from the bride's bouquet.
Often, they're somewhat smaller but echo her bouquet in the choice of flowers,
shape, colors, or other elements. The flowers for the maid or matron of honor
usually reflect those of the maids but are also distinctive: If the bridesmaids are
carrying pink roses, for example, the maid of honor might carry roses in multicolored shades of pink, from petal pale to rich scarlet, or variegated roses in deep
pink and white.

But bouquets aren't the only flower option. Some brides select wicker flower baskets for their attendants, densely packed with flowers (especially pretty in spring or summer), or woodland-style baskets nested with moss and herbs. Baskets should be light, easy to carry (especially important for the flower girl), able to stand firmly without toppling, and easily transportable. Note: While flower girls traditionally strew rose or other flower petals in the bride's path during the

Page 72: Red is the signature element in this bride's color scheme. Red is considered a deeply romantic color, and takes on special significance around holidays like Valentine's Day and Christmas. A close-up photograph of the bride's bouquet can be seen on page 58.

Opposite: The difference between the bride's bouquet and the bridesmaids' bouquets can be subtle. For this wedding, the bride's bouquet consisted of pale pink roses while the bridesmaids' posies featured darker-toned tea-colored roses.

Above: Lacy ferns and silvery Dusty Miller add a wealth of textures and colors to these two attendants' bouquets of pink snowberries and lavender roses.

Below: Bouquets for the bridesmaids take their cue from the bride's. Although smaller, they often include similar flowers, colors or other related elements.

processional, another option is to have your flower girl give a single rose to every guest sitting along the aisle.

For weddings with a period or rustic theme, bridesmaids may carry a Shakespearean-style garland of fresh flowers, and for weddings with an Elizabethan or Victorian flavor, why not consider floral pomanders for your attendants?

Floral hoops are a charming option for a young bridesmaid, flower girl, or page boy. (Hoops are often easier for children to carry than a basket.) To complement a floral hoop, flower girls and junior bridesmaids generally wear in their hair a matching flower circlet, such as an ivy vine loosely wrapped

Opposite: *Like a wedding ring, a floral circlet is a circle without beginning or end. To crown a veil, what could be prettier than this classic circlet of silken roses?*

Above: *Traditionally suspended over the spot where the bride and groom would stand together at the altar, a horseshoe made entirely of white flowers was meant to bring the couple good luck in their life together. In a modern take on the custom, this flower girl carried the horseshoe down the aisle.*

Right: *Long-stemmed pink sweet peas and paperwhites overflow from this flower girl's basket.*

WEARING FLOWERS IN YOUR HAIR

Every bride aspires to be the epitome of romance on this, her most romantic day, and nothing suggests romance as much as bedecking your hair with flowers. At the same time, wilted or browning flowers strewn throughout your hair are certainly less than lovely. So what can you do to keep the flowers you choose for your hair fresh and beautifully blooming?

If you plan to wear a headpiece adorned with flowers, such as a floral crown or a floral tiara attached to the veil (or even used without a veil), the best option is to have two head-pieces, one for the ceremony and pictures, another for the reception. This will ensure that the flowers stay fresh looking.

The same holds true of individual flowers woven into your coiffure. Flowers may be braided, pinned, or woven into the hair, and most florists are happy to provide a second set of flowers to reweave into the hair before the reception. (Hairstylists generally take care to arrange the flowers so they are easy to remove and replace.)

Flowers are usually wired and then taped with florist tape to make them easier to handle, although some hairstylists prefer to work with flowers in their natural state. Many prefer using smaller blooms, as they tend to last longer and it's easier to work the stems into the hair. Stephanotis, a deli-cate, white, star-shaped flower that adds an air of innocence and elegance, is a bridal favorite, as are other smaller, hardy flowers such as narcissus, daisies, smaller varieties of orchids, and spray roses or miniature roses.

Be sure to discuss with your florist the flowers you are considering for your hair; he or she is a good resource as to what types of flowers make the best hair accessories.

Getting the flowers from your florist also will ensure that they match or complement your bouquet. Blooms such as

jasmine, bulb flowers such as tulips or daffodils, and large flowers tend to wilt faster, so keep that in mind and make sure to have duplicates.

If you are planning to have a stylist do your hair, it's a good idea to do a practice run before the wedding. That way you can ensure that the style is to your liking and that you can move around, dance, etc., without the flowers falling out, as well as learn how to replace them easily if need be. Because it's always a bit disheartening to see a bedraggled bride, on the day of the wedding the bride's hair is usually done last so she looks as fresh as possible, and the flowers do too.

Another important factor to keep in mind before you put flowers in your hair: Make sure that you and your groom both find their fragrance pleasing.

Floral headpieces to consider:

Circlet—A floral wreath that nestles on top of your head or at mid-forehead.

Coronet—A floral wreath that rests high on the crown of your head.

Garden Hat—A crownless hat trimmed with flowers and ribbons.

Hair Bow—Usually made of satin or lace and positioned at the back of the head, often flower trimmed.

Headband—A raised hair band, often decorated and orna-mented with flowers.

Tiara—A type of headpiece made up of fresh or silk flowers, or a combination of both, typically held together with wire. (A fresh one will usually last a full day out of water.)

on a framework of birch twigs with flowers and berries attached. Flower girls can also wear a headband with rosebuds or pansies and lily of the valley attached and, instead of conventional flower baskets, carry miniature watering cans filled with lilies, irises, and pansies.

Far left: Using silk flowers is becoming an increasingly popular choice. They are a terrific option for your hair, because they look fresh all day.

Near left: Floral crowns are perennial favorites for flower girls. This young flower girl wears a wreath of creamy roses and rosemary.

In addition to those they carry, bridesmaids often wear their flowers, sometimes head to toe: in the crown of a wide-brimmed straw hat, attached to a silk ribbon worn

around the neck (instead of a locket or pearls), even as trim on their shoes (think of tiny rosebuds or miniature silk bachelor's buttons). Muffs trimmed in flowers or made entirely of flowers are pretty at winter weddings, and flower purses created by your florist are a charming and increasingly popular choice often favored by mothers of the bride and grooms who don't care for corsages. Other options for mothers of the bride and groom include small nosegays or flowers worn in their hair or on a head-piece, or a silk-flower ornament studded with gold or crystal beading. If a traditional, sweet-smelling corsage (usually an orchid) is worn, it's generally pinned above the left

Opposite: *If the mothers of the bride and groom do not want to wear a corsage, another option is to have them carry a small nosegay.*

Above: *Small posies are perfect for small hands. This one is composed of lilies of the valley.*

breast on a suit or covered dress, on the shoulder strap of a bare dress, attached to an evening bag or purse, or worn as a wristlet.

Boutonnieres

Boutonnieres, gallantly pinned to the left lapel of all the men in your wedding party, are worn at informal daytime weddings and formal nighttime affairs alike. Also called buttonholes, these typically are single flowers (such as white or red roses), although less conventional choices include two or three rosebuds, a sprig of freesia, or a few buds of stephanotis with a bit of ivy. Indeed, nowadays, anything goes: a sprig of white lilac, tiny roses mixed with hyacinth . . .

One old-time custom calls for the bride to pluck a flower from her bouquet and tenderly pin it to the groom's left lapel before the ceremony. Although this is seldom

Far right and near right: Two classic bouton-nieres. The groom's bou-tonniere usually reflects the flowers in the bridal bouquet and should be slightly different from those of the groomsmen in the wedding party.

observed today (most brides are too nervous), the groom's boutonniere is frequently composed of one or two of the same flowers as in the bride's bouquet and is often slightly different in appearance from those of the other men in the wedding party. Tip: If you are having your wedding pictures taken before the ceremony, ask your florist for a second boutonniere, so your groom can replace the one that may have wilted or become lackluster after greeting everyone and kissing them hello. Also, if the men in the wedding party are to wear breast-pocket handkerchiefs, boutonnieres are not worn.

Above: *A small posy of yellow roses. A yellow rose means friendship in the language of flowers.*

Left: *If the family pet will be attending the wedding, he or she can also wear flowers! The bride's bull mastiff completed the bridal party at this wedding, sporting a garland of orchids and ivy. The orchids matched the orchids used throughout the wedding site.*

CHAPTER 6

Flowers for the
Ceremony and Reception

Decorating your ceremony site with flowers adds to the beauty
and festive nature of the occasion, enhancing the sense of joy
for you, your groom, and your guests. But no two places are
alike—ceremony venues range from houses of worship, hotels,
and living rooms to galleries, lofts, parks, gardens, and more—and they don't all
have the same policies on the use of floral decorations. Some venues may not permit
additional flowers, floral altar decorations, or other adornments at all. So be sure
that you or your florist obtain any permissions required.

**Below are ideas on how to use flowers to make the site of your
ceremony special.**

Colorful floral wreaths or garlands on doors create an immediate sense of wel-
come for arriving guests. Particularly effective are seasonal touches: a wreath of
gilded pinecones and berries in winter; branches of flowering forsythia, dogwood, or

Page 84: *A simple floral accent, hydrangeas festoon the peaked roof over the entrance to this church.*

Opposite and right: *A handsome barn was the site of this reception. The floral decorations on the exterior and interior were very simple— the colors and flower varieties are the same as those in the bride's bouquet—and were accented by small twinkling lights decorating the ceiling and posts in the barn.*

cherry blossoms in spring; a sheaf of wheat for good luck in late summer or fall. Inside, enliven simple spaces with floral archways or bowers along the aisle, and matching floral arrangements on either side. Windowsills, fonts, lecterns, choir stalls, and pillars all provide opportunities for floral display.

In a large church or synagogue, consider a single, dramatic floral arrangement at the altar or, alternatively, two matching arrangements on either side of the aisle. The grander the setting, the larger and more dramatic the flowers should be; opt for long-stemmed blooms rather than small, short-stemmed blossoms, which tend to get visually lost in a large space.

Pew and chair decorations need to be carefully thought out so they don't obstruct the aisle in any way. Steer clear of anything that will block the view of the bridal procession, interfere with the flow of the bride's train, or impede the procession's

Right: Pew decorations composed of small bouquets of orchids.

Far right: Flower petals ready to hand out to guests for tossing.

walk down the aisle. If there is room, consider baskets or pots filled with flowers at the ends of the pews, or hang small garlands at the ends, to earmark those pews set aside for family members.

In putting together an at-home wedding, be as lavish with flowers as your budget permits. Hang a floral wreath on the door. Place flowers in the hallway, on stairway landings, entwined in chandeliers, on the fireplace mantel, side tables, and even in the bathrooms where guests go to freshen up. Outside, porch railings and pillars are ideal places for ivy vines and other greenery, and hanging baskets overflowing with flowers always add a festive touch.

After the ceremony, to shower the bride and groom with flower petals (instead of rice or birdseed), place petals near the doors so guests can easily take a handful as they exit. Or fill individual glassine envelopes or cones with petals and pass them around in big baskets so guests will have something to hold the petals in before tossing.

Above: *For an at-home wedding, dress up chairs with a swathe of pure-white blossoms tied with pale blue ribbon.*

Reception Flowers and Table Settings

When your guests finally walk into your reception area—be it at home or at a country club, reception hall, hotel, or some other location—you'll want quite simply to take their breath away. That's where all the weeks and months of planning and designing your flowers come in. For the most part, it's the reception flowers that truly set the mood and create the festive atmosphere for the celebration of your life.

Long before the arrival of your wedding date, your florist will have already visited the reception site (probably several times). Will pedestals or columns be needed? Are there balconies, archways, or other interesting architectural features that could be highlighted with flowers and greenery? The florist needs to decide beforehand where the flower arrangements are going to go before he or she decides to make them tall or wide, round or full. And where to slip in the touches—the fresh lemon leaves arranged in the shape of a heart and hung like a wreath on the entry door or a heart-shaped basket packed with tiny blossoms for the place-card table—that make your wedding unique.

Opposite: A blend of simplicity and sophistication: lush bouquets in fiery red and orange hues that are low enough for easy conversation.

Left: Small clay pots surrounding a white vase filled with white flowers make a charming centerpiece. The clay pots could also be used as favors for your guests.

As brides have become more knowledgeable about flowers, so wedding center-pieces and table settings are being designed with more individual flair, combining tradition with invention. So look beyond the usual bridal clichés to add a touch of surprise, glamour, or whimsy to your celebration. It could be as simple as placing sparkly little votive lights encircled by tiny flowers at each place setting. Or setting small bunches of lily of the valley, grape hyacinth, or violets in tiny bottles on a mantel. One designer delights in using different types of containers on each table—unmatched teacups, milk-glass pitchers, terra-cotta urns, silver canisters, or other unconventional objects—each holding a different type of flower, for what she calls "an at-home, residential look."

Seasonal accents can add special significance: a cornucopia of ferns, moss, pinecones, gourds, and harvest leaves together with rich-toned flowers in amber, burgundy, and russet tones for fall; winter's forest evergreens mixed with lush garnet roses; or a sparkling "wonderland" of all-white flowers paired with shimmery crystal beads in gleaming silver canisters. For spring and summer, how about combining oranges, lemons, and other fruits in arrangements with flowering branches of cherry, apple, or quince?

Below are some guidelines along with trends and tips to what's new and noteworthy:

Height: Floral arrangements should be either very high or quite low, so your guests can see each other and make conversation across the table. For rooms with high ceilings or big spaces, consider tall glass cylinders filled halfway with polished stones and holding sweeping floral branches. Or an elegant wrought-iron candelabrum with hanging votives and strewn petals at its base. For a low centerpiece, try a cluster of five or six small arrangements grouped together that guests can then take away as

Opposite: *Victorian candelabrum and towering vases adorn the dinner tables on the tented lawn at this reception. The height of each arrangement adds a dramatic touch to this sumptuous display, yet allow guests to converse with ease. All-white flowers set off with glossy greenery are massed at the candelabra bases for interest at eye level.*

favors. If you're not sure about what you've chosen, ask your florist to make up a sample and place it on the table to see if you like it.

A Tisket, a Tasket: Baskets, a perennial wedding favorite, are economical and available in countless graceful shapes. You can fill them with flowers—informal blooms such as tulips, daisies, and sweet peas are good choices for most baskets—or line them with a linen napkin and fill them with bread. Bread baskets evoke a country or harvest theme and give guests something to eat as soon as they are seated. Another option in keeping with a country or harvest theme is to fill baskets with lemons, apples, peaches, or nectarines—fruits with strong colors.

Light: Tall candelabrum centerpieces, while dramatic and beautiful, require a minimal number of flowers; they need just a few bits of greenery and blossoms around the base and some flowers entwined around the branches. Candles of all sizes and heights interspersed among vases of flowers create a look that's elegant and romantic.

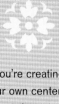

If you're creating your own center-pieces, keep in mind the florists' rule of thumb: The vase or container should be one-half to one-third the size of the total arrangement (e.g., three-foot delphiniums or gladiolus need a twelve- to eighteen-inch vase).

Opposite: *Sunflowers are a terrific choice for a summer wedding. The square metal buckets add a casual air to the table decorations and work perfectly with the checkered yellow table cloths and napkins.*

Left: *A centerpiece composed of multicol-ored roses in shades of coral-rose, peach, ivory, and pink tops a glass bowl filled with seashells—perfect for a summer wedding by the seashore. Seashells also are strewn on the table and used as napkin rings.*

Opposite: *The elegance of a monochromatic and formal table is enhanced with bunches of white blooms, including a single gardenia in a silver cup.*

Right: *A simple yet chic table setting composed of a single spray of orchids and three votive candles. The camera allows guests to take their own candid shots of the reception.*

Far right: *There are myriad ways to add a special floral touch to your reception, such as this single rose adorning a caterer's tray.*

Creative Containers: Unusual containers are increasingly popular (think pewter, silver plate, faux mother-of-pearl, or porcelain).

Mix It Up: Whimsical arrangements featuring berries, grasses, and flowers, and luscious fruits, such as blueberries, champagne grapes, figs, and even vegetables, add charm and make out-of-the-ordinary centerpieces.

Keep It Simple . . . Again: Lots of brides want simpler, smaller centerpieces. Consider floating candles amid floating flowers; or a single candle in the center of each table with rose petals sprinkled around the base.

Special Touches: Consider a different centerpiece for the bride and groom's own table; decorating the bride and groom's chairs with twisted vines, flowers, and foliage; flower ice cubes at the bar (place an edible blossom in each compartment of an ice tray, add water, and freeze; in summer, try nasturtium or mint); and floral-adorned

menus for guests (slip menus into napkins, fold, tie with a ribbon, and tuck a fresh flower into the bow).

Favorite Flowers: Exotic orchids are still many a bride's dream flower, especially the more unusual varieties. Lush, romantic hydrangeas come in a range of colors (blue, lavender, pinks, and pale greens) and elegant dahlias (clean, crisp) are showing up at fashionable weddings, as are humble carnations—a great choice for brides on a budget. In offbeat colors such as lime green or hot pink, masses of spicy little carnations tightly packed into a centerpiece look colorful, fresh, and very attractive.

Opposite: *Burgundy peonies and tulips anchor this exuberant and sophisticated arrangement.*

Above, left: *Roses, green hydrangea, and lemon leaves in silver cups adorn this bar set up at an outdoor wedding.*

Above, right: *A delicate flourish at the table— soft pink table linens are caught up with sweet peas and sprigs of lilac and tied with ivy.*

Decorating the Wedding Cake and Cake Table

Today, while still elaborately decorated, wedding cakes are more often than not crowned with fresh flowers. Fresh flowers also often decorate cake tables too.

Flowers for your wedding cake are the result of collaboration between you, your baker, and your florist. At the very least, your baker will need to give the top tier diameter measurement to your florist (usually six to eight inches). The florist then covers a plastic dish with greenery and flowers to set on top (almost like a corsage but without the pin!) and provides petals to sprinkle on and around the cake. Other options are more elaborate, taking into consideration the color of the icing, the flavor of the cake, or the wedding theme. Tiered cakes with flowers in between the tiers can also be created, with anything from blue hydrangeas to red roses—anything goes—but beware of poisonous flowers such as foxgloves or poinsettias. Consult with your florist to see which flowers are edible or nonpoisonous. In addition, it is essential that you make sure that the flowers for your cake haven't been sprayed with insecticides or other toxic materials.

Your baker must deliver the cake early enough so that the florist can decorate it properly (it can take an hour or more to decorate a large cake). Note: Even though flowers and greenery are carefully washed before being placed on the cake, all florists and bakers caution that they still should *never* be eaten.

Because the bride and groom are usually photographed with the wedding cake, the table is also often decorated. Similar decorations can be designed for the guest-book table and any other special locations at the reception.

Opposite: Remember that the wedding cake will be one of the most photographed elements of the reception. Why not make it picture perfect? Here, an array of roses, lilies, and stephanotis mixed with greenery complete the romantic look of this cake.

Above: *A few hydrangea blooms dress up this traditional white wedding cake perfectly.*

CHAPTER 7

Your Wedding Day

After months of careful preparation, the big day has arrived! In the morning, confirm with your florist when and where your flowers will arrive, and how they'll be distributed among the bridal party. Where will your wedding pictures be taken? Your florist should arrive at the site around the same time as the photographer, since you'll want to have the bouquets, boutonnieres, and corsages ready for all your photographs. Be sure to check the delivery carefully to ensure that the right flowers have been delivered and that they're in good condition. Your florist should inspect the flowers as well as soon as possible and remove any bruised or damaged petals. Have a friend or family member—someone who knows all the members of the bridal party—help the florist distribute the bridesmaids' bouquets, corsages, and boutonnieres.

Flower Delivery

On the big day, the following schedule should be followed:

2 to 3 Hours Before the Ceremony: Your reception flowers should be delivered to the reception venue for setup. (Don't forget to tip the delivery people; ask a family member or one of the bridal party members to handle this for you.)

1 to 2 Hours Before the Ceremony: The flowers should be delivered to the church or other ceremony location for setup. Make sure everyone has their bouquet, boutonniere, or corsage, and, if the flower girls and ring bearer need flowers that they have theirs, too. Bridesmaids' bouquets can be handed out just before they walk down the aisle, unless photos are being taken before the ceremony.

At the Ceremony: After greeting your fiancé at the altar, hand your bouquet to your maid of honor. She should return it to you when you head back down the aisle.

At the Reception: Traditionally, the bride's bouquet is placed on the cake table. However, the bouquet may be displayed anywhere: on the cake table; the gift, guest-book, or place-card table; or even in a vase on the head table.

Page 102: The happy day has arrived!

Above: According to tradition, the bride's bouquet is placed on the cake table. This is a nice way to decorate the cake table, and it also gives guests the opportunity to admire your bouquet close-up.

Preserving the Bride's Bouquet

Because so much thought goes into selecting a bridal bouquet, many brides choose not to toss it (or to toss a duplicate, called a "tossing bouquet") but prefer instead to preserve it as a precious romantic keepsake.

There are a number of ways to preserve fresh flowers, and it's best to consult with your florist to determine the best method for preserving the particular flowers you have chosen (he or she may be able to do it for you). Keep in mind that most flowers will darken: white flowers turn cream or ivory, and others turn brown. Also, some methods of flower preservation last longer than others; dried flowers not treated with a preserving agent, for example, may only last a few months.

If you choose to preserve your bouquet professionally, make the arrangements before the event so the process can begin as soon as possible after the celebrations— who wants to preserve a half-dead bouquet? The same applies if you're going to do it yourself: Don't wait too long. It's for this reason that some brides have the florist deliver a duplicate bouquet for preservation purposes, after they return from the honeymoon.

To keep your bouquet truest to its original form, freeze-drying is the most faithful method thus far. It takes twelve to fourteen days to complete the process and is a bit pricey ($165 to $600), but there's really no way to do it on your own. Your flowers are first treated with a

---

THE BOUQUET TOSS

Following the reception, many brides still happily participate in the bouquet toss, flinging their bouquets (or a duplicate made especially for the ritual) into a crowd of single female well-wishers, all of whom vie for the honor of catching it, thereby becoming (or so says tradition), the next woman to marry.* The origin of the custom goes back to the second half of the nineteenth century, when brides dismantled their bouquets after the wedding and presented a flower to each bridesmaid. This practice evolved into bridal bouquets actually being fashioned from numerous smaller bouquets held together with ribbons that were untied and the posies distributed to the bride's attendants. The lucky maid who received the one with a golden ring inside was heralded as the next bride-to-be.

Even though it's a long-standing tradition, some brides and their friends find the bouquet toss ritual a bit embarrassing. So they may opt to give their bouquet to someone special. If you choose to do the same, and your bouquet contains ivy, why not cut off a snippet and plant it in an ornamental pot or in your garden as a remembrance all your married days.

*The bouquet toss was also said to serve as a distraction for wedding guests, as the commotion allowed the bride and groom to "steal away" on their wedding trip without being followed.

chemical to prevent bubbles from forming and to preserve their color, then flash frozen in a special machine that draws out the moisture. Afterward, a polymer spray is applied to increase their longevity. Although the blooms are fragile, there is gener-ally minimal shrinkage as the quick drying crystallizes the blossoms, so they remain almost lifelike. Colors tend to fade slightly as the flowers age. According to experts, orchids, daisies, Asiatic lilies, and bouvardia are the least suited to this method.

Air-drying is another popular choice, and the best way to do this is to take your bouquet apart and dry the flowers separately. Tie a cotton string around the stem of each flower and hang it upside down from the ceiling in a warm, dark room. When dried (one to three weeks, depending on the type of flower), coat with a finishing spray (such as Krylon); otherwise the flowers will be too brittle. Because of the brit-tle nature of air-dried flowers, putting the bouquet back together is the most difficult part. Still, it's best not to try to hang your entire bouquet. Not only will it take a very long time to dry, but it may dry unevenly (the outer flowers drying more quickly, the inner ones staying moist); and brightly colored flowers can stain lighter ones. Other risks: Flowers may start to decompose, and if you live in an area where the humidity is high, mold can grow on the flowers.

For dehydrated flowers, air circulation is also used. It is best to purchase a dehy-drator ($100 to $200 at outdoor or camping shops or from specialty cooking cata-logs) for this method. Since most dehydrators are too small for large or even medi-um-size bouquets, experts recommend that you dehydrate each flower individually. Dehydrating is a faster method of preservation than air-drying, but you must remember to turn the flowers often so they don't get flattened on one side. If you choose to frame the bouquet in a deep shadowbox frame, this method is perfect.

For quicker results, try microwave drying. Place a layer of silica gel (available in most craft stores) in a microwave-safe glass dish, and set the timer for one minute. The silica gel will turn blue. Place the flowers on top, then add another layer of silica gel to cover the flowers completely. Microwave for one to three minutes (varies with microwave), remove the dish, and let the flowers sit for twenty to thirty minutes. Microwave drying is best for flowers with many petals and "deep forms," such as marigolds, roses, carnations, and zinnias (steer clear of flowers with thin, delicate petals or hairy, sticky surfaces). When done, the flowers should be completely dry, but if not,

apply another layer of silica gel and let them sit for five to ten additional minutes.

Besides silica gel, other desiccants can be used to dry the flowers in your bouquet, including alum or borax mixed with cornmeal (one part to two parts, respectively). To draw the moisture out of flowers with this method, spread the drying agent you've chosen in a container, and place the flowers on the agent. Daisies and other blossoms with a single row of petals should be placed bloom side down on the mixture, whereas flowers with long stalks, such as delphiniums, should be placed sideways and multipetal blooms, such as roses, can be upright. Then, add more of the drying agent over the flowers and store in a cool, dark place. Drying times vary, depending on the agent, but generally about a week will do it. When the flowers are completely dry, brush them with a soft paintbrush or makeup brush to remove any remaining mixture.

Although glycerin does not work well with most flowers, it does work beautifully on greenery and baby's breath. Here's how: Add glycerin to hot tap water in a vase or other container, one part to two parts, respectively. Then smash the stem of whatever foliage you are drying and place it in the mixture for up to three weeks. The mix-

Above: Special touches marked this romantic garden wedding, including a floral collar for a winsome cat sculpture.

ture can be reused, and the material you've preserved should be stored in a cool, dry place. This is one method that does not cause the foliage to become brittle.

For pressed flowers, your best bet is to use a simple flower press, which can be purchased in a craft store or easily made at home. (To make a press, take two pieces of wood and with a screw and bolt, fasten at each corner. Use pliers to tighten and loosen the bolts as needed.) A couple of very large, heavy books can be used as well.

When laying out the flowers, make sure to use paper (blotting paper or even typing paper works well) between the layers of flowers to absorb moisture and any stains that the flowers may produce. Place the paper between each layer so flowers don't touch the ones above or below. The flowers are essentially flattened but will retain some shape and, occasionally, the impression of the flower being pressed above or below it. Let them sit for five to six weeks—a longer drying process ensures better color retention, but most flowers will be darkened, muted, or browned.

To simply preserve the essence of the bouquet, potpourri is a lovely option. The best way to dry the leaves and petals of the flowers is to use a dehydrator, although you can also use the air-dry method, placing them in a flat basket or on a screen. Separate the petals and leaves, then cover with cheesecloth to protect them from dust and dirt and let them sit until dry. Add a few drops of essential oil like lavender or lemon balm, and mix. Place in a sealed glass jar and shake occasionally to mature scent. It's a practical and useful way to keep your bouquet around for years to come.

If you choose to preserve your bouquet professionally, make the arrangements before the event so the process can begin as soon as possible after the celebrations—who wants to preserve a half-dead bouquet?

Acknowledgments

We would like to gratefully acknowledge all those whose knowledge, editorial assistance, and photographs have contributed to this book. Their input has been invaluable, and we thank them:

Christa Weber, AKL Studio, NYC; Tom and Dennis at Ariston Florists, NYC; Francis De La Hoz, hairstylist, Devachan Salon, NYC; Kathy Reid at Heller & Reid Bridal Bouquet Preservation, Richardson, Texas; Monica at Beers Flower Shop, Ridgewood, NJ; Inna at City Blossoms, NYC; Anthony Rodriguez at Fellan Florist, NYC; the wedding consultants at Marcy Blum Associates, NYC; Wendy Kraus at Bloom, NYC; Special Events Consultant Susan Chagnon, NYC; Stuart Brownstein at Colin Cowie Lifestyle, NYC; wedding consultant Corinne Strauss of Hampton

Weddings, NY; Annie at Annie & Co. Silk Flowers, Vancouver; Nic Faitos at Starbright Floral Designs, NYC; Gerard Musella at Richard Salome Flowers Inc., NYC; Luis Collazo at Lotus Florists; Bobbi Hicks of Weddings by Bobbi, Sarasota, FL; and Gabriella at Ferrara Café, NYC.

Photography Credits

Page 2: Mallory Samson
Page 6: Toshi Otsuki
Page 8: Luciana Pampalone
Page 10: Toshi Otsuki
Page 12: Toshi Otsuki
Page 18: David Prince
Page 21: Toshi Otsuki
Page 23: David Prince
Page 25: Wendi Schneider
Page 27: Starr Ockenga
Page 28: David Prince
Page 31 (left): Toshi Otsuki

Page 31 (right): Toshi Otsuki
Page 33: Luciana Pampalone
Page 34: Jana Taylor
Page 36 (Amaryills):
  John Glover
Page 36 (Anemone): Marlene
  Wetherell
Page 36 (Aster): John Glover
Page 36 (Calla Lily): John Glover
Page 37 (Camellia): John Glover
Page 37 (Canterbury Bells):
  John Glover

Page 37 (Chrysanthemum):
  John Glover
Page 37 (Cosmos): John Glover
Page 37 (Cornflower):
  John Glover
Page 38 (Dutch Tulip): Minh
  and Wass
Page 39 (Daffodil): John Glover
Page 39 (Dahlia): Marina Schinz
Page 39 (Daisy): John Glover
Page 39 (Delphinium):
  John Glover

Page 39 (Forget-Me-Not): John Glover
Page 39 (Freesia): Toshi Otsuki
Page 39 (French Tulip): John Glover
Page 39 (Gardenia): John Glover
Page 40 (Gerbera Daisy): John Glover
Page 40 (Gladiolus): John Glover
Page 40 (Grape Hyacinth): John Glover
Page 40 (Hyacinth): John Glover
Page 40 (Hydrangea): John Glover
Page 40 (Iris): John Glover
Page 40 (Lilac): John Glover
Page 40 (Lily): Toshi Otsuki
Page 41 (Lily of the Valley): David Prince
Page 42 (Orchid): John Glover
Page 42 (Peony): David Prince
Page 42 (Phlox): John Glover
Page 42 (Ranunculus): Jennifer Jordan
Page 42 (Rose): Elizabeth Zeschin
Page 43 (Stephanotis): John Glover
Page 43 (Sunflower): John Glover
Page 43 (Sweet Pea): David Prince
Page 43 (Veronica): John Glover
Page 43 (Zinnia): John Glover
Page 43: Mallory Samson
Page 46: Luciana Pampalone
Page 47: Toshi Otsuki
Page 48: David Prince
Page 49: Wendi Schneider
Page 51: Mallory Samson
Page 52: William Meppem
Page 55: David Prince
Page 58: William Meppem
Page 60: Mallory Samson
Page 61 (top): Toshi Otsuki
Page 61 (bottom): Luciana Pampalone
Page 62 (top): Toshi Otsuki
Page 62 (bottom): Toshi Otsuki
Page 63: Mallory Samson
Page 64 (left): Thomas Hooper
Page 64 (right): Thomas Hooper
Page 65: Mallory Samson
Page 66: Mallory Samson
Page 67 (left): Laura Rosen

Page 67 (right): Jana Taylor
Page 68 (left): Toshi Otsuki
Page 68 (right): Jana Taylor
Page 70: Toshi Otsuki
Page 71: Toshi Otsuki
Page 72: William Meppen
Page 74 (top): Toshi Otsuki
Page 74 (bottom): Toshi Otsuki
Page 75: Toshi Otsuki
Page 76 (top): Toshi Otsuki
Page 76 (bottom): Wendi Schneider
Page 77: Toshi Otsuki
Page 79 (top): Toshi Otsuki
Page 79 (bottom): Toshi Otsuki
Page 80: William Meppem
Page 81: David Prince
Page 82 (left): Mallory Samson
Page 82 (right): William Meppem
Page 83 (top): Toshi Otsuki
Page 83 (bottom): Toshi Otsuki
Page 84: Toshi Otsuki
Page 86: William Meppem
Page 87: William Meppem
Page 88 (left): William Meppem
Page 88 (right): William Meppem
Page 89: Toshi Otsuki
Page 90: Mallory Samson
Page 91: Courtesy of *Victoria* Magazine
Page 93: Toshi Otsuki
Page 94: Mallory Samson
Page 95: Toshi Otsuki
Page 96 (left): William Meppem
Page 96 (right): Toshi Otsuki
Page 97: Mallory Samson
Page 98: David Montgomery
Page 99 (left): Toshi Otsuki
Page 99 (right): Toshi Otsuki
Page 100: Mallory Samson
Page 101: Toshi Otsuki
Page 102: Toshi Otsuki
Page 104: Toshi Otsuki
Page 107: Toshi Otsuki

Index